St Luke and the Church of Jerusalem

by
G. W. H. LAMPE

D.D., F.B.A.

*Ely Professor of Divinity
in the University of Cambridge*

The Ethel M. Wood Lecture
delivered before the University of London
on 4 March 1969

UNIVERSITY OF LONDON
THE ATHLONE PRESS
1969

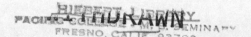

Published by
THE ATHLONE PRESS
UNIVERSITY OF LONDON
at 2 Gower Street, London WC1

Distributed by Tiptree Book Services Ltd
Tiptree, Essex

Australia and New Zealand
Melbourne University Press

Canada
Oxford University Press
Toronto

U.S.A.
Oxford University Press Inc
New York

485 14314 3

Printed in Great Britain by
WESTERN PRINTING SERVICES LTD
BRISTOL

ST LUKE AND THE CHURCH OF
JERUSALEM

Matthew, we were taught at school, is the Gospel for the Jews, and Luke is the Gospel addressed to the Gentiles, with Acts as a sort of appendix to Luke's Gospel, added to it in order to tell us how the Church began and how Paul converted the Gentile world. Most of us, I imagine, were therefore surprised when we came to read these books for ourselves more attentively. The Gentile Gospel ends with the Lord commanding the eleven to stay in the city of Jerusalem, and the last words of the story are that 'they were continually in the Temple blessing God'. Nothing could be less 'Gentile'. On the other hand the ending of the supposedly Jewish Gospel is a command of the Lord to the eleven, given not in Jerusalem but on a Galilean mountain, to go and make disciples of all the nations, or all the Gentiles.

The beginning of the two Gospels is as surprising as their ending. Matthew's infancy narrative mentions Jerusalem only as Herod's capital to which the magi come and which they throw into confusion by the news they bring. The Holy Family never go there. Such action as does not take place in Bethlehem happens far away in Gentile Egypt or at Nazareth in Galilee of the Gentiles. But the 'Gentile' Gospel opens in the heart of Jerusalem where a Jewish priest is carrying out his ritual duties in the Temple. The central episode in Luke's infancy narrative is the Presentation: the coming of the Lord's Messiah to the Temple, the revelation to Simeon of God's salvation, and the testimony to this given by Anna to all those who were awaiting the redemption of Jerusalem. Luke's stories of the birth and infancy of the Baptist and Jesus move from Jerusalem to Galilee, to 'a city of Judah' where the Jerusalem priest Zacharias and his wife live, back, after a momentary return with Mary to Galilee after the Visitation, to the hill country of Judaea for the birth of John, to Bethlehem for the Nativity, to Jerusalem for the Presentation, and to the Temple once more for the one disclosure in the 'hidden years': the picture of Jesus in the Temple, as the son of God in his Father's house—a picture in which are foreshadowed Jesus' teaching in the Temple, and his questionings and disputings with the scribes, chief priests and Sadducees after his expulsion of the traders; a picture, too, which prefigures the three days of his absence from his people at another Passover time.

An intense interest in Jerusalem is characteristic of the early part, not of Matthew but of Luke the 'Gentile'. Of course, his concern with Jerusalem and the Temple in the opening chapters of his first volume is often contrasted with the complete change of scene to which his second volume leads us. From an Old Testament priest offering incense in the Temple, with the people of Israel praying outside, we are taken by way of Galilee, the journey of Jesus to Jerusalem for his 'assumption', and the Spirit-empowered mission of the apostolic Church, to the very heart of the Gentile world: to Paul in Rome, receiving all comers in his house, proclaiming the kingdom of God and teaching about the Lord Jesus Christ, with all boldness of speech, unhindered. The theme seems to be 'How we brought the good news from Jerusalem to Rome'.

Yet it is precisely there, in Rome, that Luke gives us another surprise. We expect Paul to receive a Roman triumph: the victory march of his great campaign from Jerusalem through all those scenes of dramatic struggle and glorious success, Antioch, Philippi, Corinth, Ephesus.

Luke seems to be preparing something on these lines. He knows that Paul's approach along the Appian Way is a great moment. 'And thus we came to Rome.' But (first anticlimax) this is not, after all, going to be a great missionary assault on the heartland of paganism. The good news has already *been* brought to Rome by persons unknown. There is a church here already; the brethren escort Paul on his way and encourage him. If we had no *Letter to the Romans* we should certainly never have expected from Luke's narrative to find a church established in Rome before Paul ever set foot there.

Stranger still (second anticlimax), Luke tells us almost nothing about the good news being proclaimed to any Romans. He does say that Paul kept open house for all comers; but that is not a very stirring description of a great evangelistic crusade. It comes, too, in what is evidently meant to be a rather sober and quiet ending to Luke's great work. This brief description of Paul preaching and teaching in his hired house corresponds to the last sentence or two of Luke's first volume: 'They were continually in the Temple blessing God' is another quiet ending. Both these passages are important. Luke 24:53 shows that the Temple has become the centre of the life and worship of the risen Christ's chosen witnesses, with the hope that from that centre the preaching of repentance and forgiveness will go out to the nations. Acts 28:30–31 tells us that the good news brought by Jesus, the gospel of God's kingdom, and the teaching of the witnesses to his Messiahship, were being proclaimed without hindrance in Rome—with the promise that here was to be a new focal point of the world-wide mission. Yet the real dramatic climax of each volume precedes these relatively tame summaries. It comes in the words (Luke 24:44–49) in which the Lord declares that in the Messiah's suffering and resurrection the ancient scriptures have been fulfilled, and commissions the apostles as witnesses to the nations,

beginning from Jerusalem. It comes in Paul's final denunciation of the Jewish leaders and his solemn turning to the Gentiles for the momentous and symbolical third time, which
leaves the Jews no further chance.

Luke tells of no dramatic conversions at Rome. Having
brought his hero to his goal, what Luke does is to turn our
attention back to Jerusalem, the starting-point. It is the
Jewish leaders whom Paul sends for on his arrival in the Gentile capital. What follows is Paul's main apologia to the
Jews. To them he introduces himself as a prisoner from
Jerusalem, one who had been handed over, like Jesus, into
the hands of Romans who hold him to be innocent and, but
for Jewish malice, would have released him. He defends his
loyalty to Israel and its traditions. The gospel which brought
him into captivity is the hope of Israel. The whole of Paul's
controversy at Rome lies within the framework of Judaism.
Not the Gentile world, but the chief men of the Jews, are
being confronted with the good news in Rome, as they have
been, up and down the world, ever since the first preaching
of Jesus in the synagogues. This is their last chance, the
final show-down. And in a whole day spent in solemnly
'declaring the kingdom of God', and 'persuading about
Jesus' by appealing to the Law and the Prophets, Paul suc-
ceeds only in creating dissension among his hearers. So, as
the real conclusion of his two volumes, Luke puts into Paul's
mouth Isaiah's tremendous denunciation: 'Go to this people
and say: You will hear and hear, but never understand; you
will look and look, but never see. For this people has grown
gross at heart; their ears are dull, their eyes are closed.
Otherwise, their eyes might see, their ears hear, and their
heart understand, and then they might turn again, and I
would heal them.'[1] Luke has already anticipated this condemnation. He followed Mark in applying Isaiah's prophecy

[1] *New English Bible* © 1961 by permission of Oxford and Cambridge
University Presses.

to those who could not understand Jesus' parables (Luke 8:10); but there he abbreviated it to the bare minimum, omitting the hardening of the people's heart—which Matthew, who greatly expanded Mark's citation, included in his Gospel at that point. The Fourth Gospel (12:37–40) refers the same prophecy to the continuing unbelief of the Jews after Jesus' ministry of signs. Luke, after partially reproducing it from Mark, keeps it until the end of the whole story: the end of the apostolic mission; and then he quotes it even more fully than Matthew. For now at Rome the prophecy is at last completely fulfilled, leaving Paul free to say: 'Be it known to you that this salvation of God has been sent to the Gentiles: *they* will listen.'

Paul's work, as Luke sees it, ends with the discharge of his responsibility towards the Jews. Though he was the apostle of the Gentiles, Luke makes it clear that he was the apostle of the Jews first. For Luke there are not two missions, to the Jews under the leadership of James or Peter and under Paul to the Gentiles. There is only one mission, with a double aim: the conversion of Israel and the drawing into Israel of a people chosen by God, paradoxically enough, from the Gentiles, as the prophets had foretold (Acts 14:15ff.). Paul was, indeed, sent far from Jerusalem to the Gentiles (Acts 22:21), but this commission, which, Luke tells us, Paul received from the Lord at Jerusalem in a vision in the Temple, did not imply any withdrawal from the Jewish side of the mission. On the contrary. For instance, if Luke found any information about Titus in his sources he kept that uncircumcised Gentile out of his picture. Paul could not have such a man as a missionary colleague, any more than he could have had Timothy, the uncircumcised son of an apostatizing marriage, without first circumcising him. Paul, as he himself told Agrippa, was sent both to 'the people' and to the Gentiles. If he turned to the Gentiles only, he did so because he was driven to it, confident in the knowledge that he had done his best for the Jews; the responsibility was theirs. So at Antioch he invokes the threatening prophecy of Habakkuk 1:5: 'See this, you scoffers, wonder, and begone; for I am doing a deed in your days, a deed which you will never believe when you are told of it'; and in Corinth he claims, in the spirit of the prophet on his watchtower: 'Your blood be on your own head; I am clean' (Acts 18:6). It is partly, at least, to this discharge of his obligation towards the Jews that he alludes in his address to the Ephesian elders: 'I am clean from the blood of all men' (Acts 20:26). At Rome this obligation comes to an end. The rejection of his message by the Jews there is the third decisive moment, rather reminiscent of the three denials of Peter, the threefold verdict of acquittal pronounced by Pilate, and the three assertions of Paul's innocence by the Pharisee scribes, Festus, and Agrippa.

The reason why in Luke's view the gospel events extend from the annunciation of the forerunner at Jerusalem to Paul's preaching in Rome is partly because the gospel is the story not only of the light of the Gentiles and the glory of Israel, but also of that 'standing or falling of many in Israel' which Simeon, probably using the Isaianic imagery of the stone of stumbling, had prophesied; and the piercing sword of which he spoke did not accomplish the division between Israelites who stood and Israelites who fell until the climax of the mission had been reached both in Jerusalem and in Rome.

There the Gospel ends. For in it Luke has grappled, like Paul in Rom. 9–11, with the problem of Israel. 'Has God rejected his people?'. Paul could answer μὴ γένοιτο, 'I cannot believe it', as the New English Bible rather tamely translates him. No: Israel had been temporarily blinded until the Gentiles should have been admitted in full strength. Then, provoked to emulation, all Israel would in turn be saved. Luke cannot say this sort of thing. He does not hope for the conversion of all Israel. The break with the synagogue is com-

plete. Jerusalem has fallen and is being trodden down by the
Gentiles (Luke 21:24). She did not know the time of her
visitation (Luke 19:44); the king of the parable of the
pounds has taken vengeance on those who would not have
him to reign over them (Luke 19:27). Had Luke thought
that the Jewish leaders had been offered any further chance
after the point where he laid down his pen, he would have
had to write a third volume to complete his theme (not to
record Paul's fate, for the Miletus speech has already alerted
the reader to the prospect that Paul is to be a martyr, and
Paul's actual condemnation would not seem important to
Luke. Nor would it embarrass him; he is not writing an
apology for Paul to the secular authority; he has told us that
every Gentile authority believed Paul to be innocent; his
death would be only a by-product of the final rejection of the
gospel by the Jews who were the sole cause of Paul's trials
and death). Thus Luke cannot hope that the conversion of
the Gentiles will provoke the Jews to emulation. Nor can he
take up an attitude like that of *Barnabas* and virtually deny
that the Jews as a whole ever were the true people of God.
Luke's position is intermediate. There has been a final rejection of a part of Israel, but this part is not, and never has
been, the authentic people of the covenant, for they have
continually broken it. From the beginning, as Stephen's
speech is meant to show, there have been two 'successions' in
Israel. The faithful and true succession passed from Abraham, Isaac and Jacob to Joseph, Moses, 'our fathers' in the
desert wanderings and the entry into Canaan, David, and on
to the Righteous One, the prophet like Moses. To this
tradition belong the covenant and the promises of God, the
living oracles, the angel of the divine presence, the tent of
witness, the prophets and, by implication, Jesus the prophet
like Moses, the promised blessings of the kingdom of God
which are repentance and forgiveness, and the witness of the
Holy Spirit. The leaders in this succession are wanderers

and exiles, men who, like Joseph and Moses, were rejected, whom God vindicated and exalted and who performed wonders and signs. The whole line leads to Jesus and the community which has been baptized in his name and possessed by the Holy Spirit. It is not a new Israel, but identical with the true succession of the covenant people. For Luke does not know of any new covenant (Luke 22:20, in the longer text of the words of Institution, is, I think, unlikely to be authentically Lucan). Rather, for Luke, the beginning of the gospel means that God has remembered his holy covenant which he made with Abraham (Luke 1:72), and the glorification of Jesus has fulfilled God's promise to Abraham for those who, as faithful Israelites, are 'the sons of the covenant which God made with the patriarchs' (Acts 3:25). This true succession is the larger part of Israel. In Luke the people, as opposed to the rulers, are friendly to Jesus and his missionaries. Luke 23:13 appears to offer an exception, but it is possible that the text is corrupt.

Stephen's other, parallel, succession is a long line of rebellion, apostasy, and persecution of the righteous: from the brothers who sold Joseph into Egypt, through the brethren of Moses who drove him into Midian, the rebels in the desert who told Aaron to make the calf, the worshippers of the host of heaven, and, though this is less clear, Solomon, who replaced the tent of testimony with a house made with hands (one may compare the derogatory use of this term at Isa. 16:12). In this succession there stand the persecutors of the prophets, and now the betrayers and murderers of the Righteous One. This 'Remnant in reverse', as it were, now, as always, resists that Holy Spirit by whose testimony the true Israel lives—the genuine covenant people into which, as Luke sees it, the Gentiles have entered, in accordance with the ancient prophecies, to replace those who were 'uncircumcised in hearts and ears' (Acts 7:51).

For Luke the question of the relation of the Church to

Israel did not involve the great Pauline problems of the Law. The accusations against Stephen and Paul, of subverting the Law, were false; indeed, the Law stands (Luke 16:17), but its main function is to be part of the prophetic witness, terminated by John the Baptist, which pointed towards the good news of the kingdom of God. But the false Israel never kept the Law (Acts 7:53), and in any case the Law was inadequate: by Jesus, through whom forgiveness of sins is proclaimed, every believer is justified in all those respects in which justification was not available by the Law of Moses (Acts 13:38). In any case, its practical demands have been relaxed since the Holy Spirit's descent upon uncircumcised Gentiles, supported by the testimony of the prophets, has proved that, as Peter said to Cornelius, God-fearers and righteous men in every nation are acceptable to God, Law or no Law (Acts 10:34).

Luke himself, and the Gentile Church of his day, have left the problem of the Law far behind in the past. He can even, perhaps forgetting for the moment about historical verisimilitude, make Peter speak of circumcision and observance of the Law as a yoke 'which neither our fathers nor we could carry' (Acts 15:10). Yet, as Luke thinks about the original mission it seems to him most important that its leaders, men in the true Israelite succession, faithful to the covenant, chosen to witness for the Messiah to the people and rulers of Israel, should themselves be devoted observers of the Law. Stephen was accused of blaspheming against Moses and God, of continually speaking against Temple and Law. But this was said by false witnesses, and Stephen's complaint about the Law is simply that the Jewish leaders, the false Israel, have never kept it. Peter was so scrupulously observant that it required a major demonstration of the divine will to convince him that God had cleansed the, legally speaking, defiled and unclean Gentiles. Luke's great concern is to vindicate Paul as a model of Jewish piety. He admits that vast numbers of Jewish Christians had been instructed (κατηχήθησαν, Acts 21:21) that Paul taught the Diaspora Jews to apostatize from Moses, not to circumcise their children, and to give up the Jewish way of life. His extreme anxiety to defend Paul's reputation as a devout Israelite suggests that this was a live issue in his own day. Is Luke defending the identity of the Church with the authentic Israel against Jewish propaganda? One recalls Justin's assertion that the Jews had mounted an anti-Christian counter-mission, based on Jerusalem: 'You chose selected men from Jerusalem and sent them out into all the world, saying that a godless sect of Christians had appeared, and recounting what all who do not know us are accustomed to say against us' (*Dialogue with Trypho*, 17.1). Or, may Luke have wanted to clear Paul's name from Ebionite slanders, such as are reflected in the Clementine literature? Or, on the other hand, is Luke defending the Church's continuity with Israel on the opposite front, against attempts, in the Marcionite manner, to deny all connection between them? However this may be, Luke forestalls the accusations made in Acts 21:21 by telling us how Paul circumcised Timothy, took a vow at Cenchreae and hurried thence to Jerusalem, presumably to discharge it; how he again hastened to Jerusalem after his last missionary journey so as to keep the Jewish Pentecost there, how on his arrival he demonstrated, at James' request, his respectability as one who 'walked so as to observe the Law' by accompanying to the Temple four men who were under a vow, paying for their sacrifices, and, for some reason which Luke does not explain, purifying himself (possibly by way of decontamination after coming from heathen lands).

Paul was accused in the riot in the Temple of teaching against People, Law and Temple (Acts 21:28); and the main burden of the last quarter or so of Acts is that, on the contrary, Paul was the most zealous devotee of Israel's religion whom one could possibly conceive; and, just for that reason, one who could rightly challenge Israel's leaders to see in the gospel, and in the gathering in of the Gentiles, the fulfilment of all that was good in their ancient tradition. This is the main thrust of Paul's apology to the Jerusalem mob, addressed as though, like Stephen's defence, it were meant for the Sanhedrin: 'Men, brethren, and fathers' (Acts 22:1). He had always been a zealous Jew; to this the high priest and all the Sanhedrin would testify, for from them (does Luke forget it was not from the same high priest?) he had obtained his commission to the brethren at Damascus ('brethren' meaning not Christians but synagogue officials). Ananias, too, at Damascus, had been a devout man according to the Law, attested as such by all the local Jews, and Ananias declared to Paul nothing revolutionary, but rather the will of 'the God of our fathers'. That Paul should become a missionary to the Gentiles was due solely to the command of the Lord who appeared to him in a trance at prayer in the Temple in Jerusalem.

To the Sanhedrin Paul presents himself as a Pharisee. The issue on which he is charged is no more than an internal Jewish dispute about resurrection. And, although Paul is charged before Felix with offences similar to those alleged against Jesus in Pilate's court, he defends himself as one who serves the God of Israel's fathers according to the Way, believing the Law and the prophets, hoping for the resurrection, and as the victim of an unprovoked attack while he was actually engaged in the good works of Jewish piety—almsgiving and sacrifice—within the Temple. The apology before Agrippa develops the same picture: of Paul as the ideal Pharisee, both before and, still more, after his conversion; and it is this repeated apology to the Jews that occupies most of Luke's story of Paul in Rome. Tedious as it all is to the casual reader of Acts, it is a dominant theme of the book. The Church, for Luke, must have been identical at the outset with the true adherents of the Mosaic covenant.

'Jerusalem and the Temple, a prominent and continuing concern of Luke':[1] so Paul Minear described it in a recent essay on the Lucan birth narratives; and this is true. But Luke sees the Temple in two aspects. It is the place where the promise of the gospel is first announced. It is visited by Jesus four times: at the Presentation, when the Messiah, bringing glory to Israel, appropriately comes into the place where God had set his Name and his glory tabernacled (for Luke readily associates the divine glory with the person of Jesus: one may note Luke 9:26, and, in contrast with the other evangelists, in the Transfiguration story, Luke 9:31–32); the second visit is to his Father's house; the third is for the climax, according to Luke, of the Temptations; and on the last visit Jesus moves straight from his royal welcome into Jerusalem to occupy the Temple, cleanse it, and within its precincts to confront the leaders of Israel with the choice of acceptance or rejection. It is the place where the first volume of Luke's gospel ends, with the nucleus of the true Israel of the Messiah's followers gathered in it to bless God for his exaltation of Jesus as the Christ. It is the scene, too, of the proclamation of the gospel, and the challenge to believe and repent, delivered by the apostles to the leaders of Israel by word and by wonders and signs. Did Luke perhaps think of it, so long as it remained the scene of the apostolic witness, as being still, and in a new sense, the 'tabernacle of testimony' spoken of by Stephen? It is the place, too, where Paul goes to demonstrate his loyalty to the Law and where his near-lynching by the mob marks the rejection of the gospel in the Temple and by the Temple's authorities. Stephen and Paul were accused of attacking the Temple, and in the charge against the former Luke refers indirectly to the fact recorded by the other evangelists that Jesus himself had been accused of threatening to destroy it. Luke insists that

[1] Paul S. Minear, 'Luke's Use of the Birth Stories', in L. E. Keck and J. L. Martyn, *Studies in Luke–Acts* (SPCK, 1968) pp. 111–30.

all this was false; and he suppresses all that Mark says directly about the alleged saying of Jesus that he would destroy the Temple and build another not made with hands.

On the other hand, Luke is well aware that the Temple is no more: the same Temple in which the Messiah had been revealed, where Jesus had taught daily, where in the early morning the people had flocked to listen to him, where the apostles had delivered their proclamation to Israel, and to which the angel who opened their prison doors had sent them back to 'stand in the Temple and speak to Israel ('the people') all the words of this Life'. Like Matthew, Luke records Jesus' words in his lament over Jerusalem, 'Look, there is your Temple, forsaken by God'; he reproduces the Marcan prophecy that not one stone will be left upon another; and, like Matthew, he omits the continuation of 'My house shall be called a house of prayer'. It cannot be 'for all the nations'. The Gentiles cannot come to the Temple for the Temple has gone. Once Israel's leaders have rejected the Messiah and his witnesses, their Temple is forsaken. It is no longer needed; for the interconnection of 'glory' and 'Spirit' in Luke's theology, and of both with Christ and so with the Church, is such that the Temple as the focal point of the divine presence and the link between heaven and earth can be supplanted.

It is against this background that Luke's rather puzzling picture of the Christian church of Jerusalem can best be understood. Luke sees Jerusalem as the place of God's decisive acts and the place where witness is borne to them: the central focus of revelation and mission. At the Transfiguration Luke tells us of the 'exodus' which Jesus is to accomplish at Jerusalem (Luke 9:31). He arranges more than a third of his Gospel in the framework of a journey on which Jesus, having 'set his face to go to Jerusalem' (Luke 9:51) for his 'assumption' through suffering and death, goes up, accompanied by the witnesses whom he had chosen in

Galilee (for 'beginning from Galilee' characterizes the ministry of Jesus, as 'beginning from Jerusalem' does that of the
apostles: cf. Luke 23:5; Acts 10:37; Luke 24:47. Those
who, like the women of Luke 23:49, 55; 24:6, went up
from Galilee to Jerusalem, witnessed Jesus' death and could
testify to his resurrection, are the ultimate guarantors of the
gospel. Paul himself has to appeal to their authority in his
Antioch speech (Acts 13:31)). In this central section of
Luke's Gospel the reader is informed three times of the
journey and of Jerusalem as its goal (Luke 9:51; 13:22;
17:11), just as in the last chapters of Acts one is told three
times that Rome is the goal set before Paul (Acts 19:21;
23:11; 27:24). The three Lucan lamentations over Jerusalem help to make the outcome clear (Luke 13:34–35 (Q);
19:41–44, and 23:28ff., both peculiar to Luke). Jesus was
greeted, according to Luke, as king, with allusion to Zecha-
riah 9:9, and possibly with Zephaniah 3:15 also in mind:
'The king of Israel, the Lord in thy midst': but Jesus is to
suffer the typical fate of every prophet at Jerusalem. He will
be handed over to the Romans, and put to death—like Paul
later on; and the consequence of the rejection by the Jerusalem authorities of the Christ and his gospel will be the
siege and destruction of the city. It will be trodden down by
the Gentiles.

But this will not happen until the apostolic mission has
fully brought about the standing and falling of many in
Israel. First, Jerusalem, where Jesus taught and died and
rose and where he commissioned his witnesses, must be the
scene of their testimony. They are told by the risen Lord
not to leave Jerusalem. Everything in the Resurrection-
Ascension-Pentecost event happens in or very near Jerusalem. To make this absolutely clear Luke drastically alters
Mark's account of the angelic message to the women at the
tomb. Luke will have no going into Galilee by the eleven and
their associates.

According to Luke 24:47, the proclamation to all nations, 'beginning from Jerusalem' is among those things that stand written in the scriptures. If this means that the place of Jerusalem in relation to the mission was foretold by the prophets, the allusion may be to Micah 4:1–3 (Isa. 2:2–4). This prophecy speaks of the nations going up to the mountain of the Lord, 'because the Law shall go forth out of Zion, and the word of the Lord from Jerusalem'. This passage is quoted in full by Justin (*Dialogue with Trypho*, 109. 1–3) and applied to the proclamation of the gospel to the Gentiles by Christ's apostles from Jerusalem. It is not actually cited by Luke but Justin has probably expressed what is implicit in Luke's narrative. With it, perhaps, Luke may have had in mind another passage, Psalm 2:6, which runs in the LXX: 'But I was set by him upon Zion his holy mountain, proclaiming the Lord's decree. The Lord said to me, "Thou art my son, today have I begotten thee; ask of me, and I will give thee the nations (or the Gentiles) for thine inheritance, and the farthest parts of the earth for thy possession".' An earlier part of the Psalm is applied to the Passion of Christ in Acts 4:25–28, and 'ask of me and I will give thee the nations . . .' is added by the Western text to the citation of 'Thou art my son . . .' as a Christological proof-text at Acts 13:33. The thought of this whole passage may well underlie the Lord's commissioning of the apostles as witnesses (Acts 1:8), although there the phrase 'the end of the earth' more directly echoes another Old Testament text, Isaiah 49:6. Further, the prophecy of Joel, which in Peter's Pentecost speech breaks off at 'whoever shall call on the name of the Lord shall be saved', continues: 'because in mount Zion and in Jerusalem there shall be one who is restored, as the Lord has said, and men to whom good news is proclaimed (εὐαγγελιζόμενοι) whom the Lord has called' (Joel 2:32). The last words of this verse actually form the conclusion of Peter's speech (Acts 2:39); and it is very possible that the whole prophecy was in Luke's mind. In any case, he had no lack of scriptural grounds for his belief that Jerusalem must be both the Church's birthplace (or rather, the place of Israel's renewal by the Spirit as the true messianic people of the last days), and also the centre and headquarters of its witness to the whole world. The constituting of the Jerusalem church in the persons of the apostles and their commissioning to witness successively in Jerusalem, Judaea, Samaria, and the end of the earth (Acts 1:8) is the mode by which in God's time the kingdom will be restored to Israel in a new form (Acts 1:6): the way in which the twelve apostles will exercise the kingdom covenanted to them at the Last Supper, and judge the twelve tribes of Israel (Luke 22:29f.). Like the nobleman in the parable, Jesus has gone to a far country to receive his kingdom. He has ascended, and Luke knows that he will not soon return, though Israel's repentance would bring the promised restoration nearer (Acts 3:19–21). In the meantime his rule is exercised from Jerusalem over the nations by the agency of the witnesses whom he designated and the testimony of the Holy Spirit which he has bestowed on them from heaven.

In the beginning the Christian Church *is* the church of Jerusalem. Later the Church spreads through the world outside Jerusalem, but always, because of its nature as the authentic and renewed Israel, this expansion takes the form of an extension of the Jerusalem church. This does not mean that Luke believes that the mission was everywhere directly organized and pioneered by Jerusalem. On the contrary, Luke makes it perfectly clear that he realizes that he has omitted to tell us about the foundation and early history of churches in many parts of the world, including Rome itself; and there is no reason to think that he believed them all to owe their origin to the direct initiative of Jerusalem. He does, however, hold that these churches all came in due course under the supervision and guidance of the church of Jerusalem.

The reason why Jerusalem must be the directing centre is, first, that the original members of that church are the apostles, which for Luke means the Twelve, and their immediate associates. This fact is emphasized by the repetition of the names of the apostles at Acts 1:13–14, the mention there also of the women who had come up with Jesus from Galilee, the momentary reappearance of Mary, the mother of Jesus, and the introduction of his brothers for the first time, apart from a brief reference to them at Luke 8:19–20. These were the original Galilean witnesses, described as Galileans up to the moment of the withdrawal of the bodily presence of the Lord. Now they become witnesses in the first instance to the people and leaders of Israel; hence the necessity that by direct divine selection, the number of the Twelve should be made up. Secondly, the church at Jerusalem is a group directly inspired for its missionary witness to the great deeds of God ($\mu\epsilon\gamma\alpha\lambda\epsilon\hat{\iota}\alpha$, Acts 2:11) through the theophany in which its first members became filled with Holy Spirit—a gift which was extended through them to the three thousand converts who received baptism. This church was thus marked out as a community of the new age, for whom the eschatological promise of the Spirit had been fulfilled; and Luke's idealizing picture of the Jerusalem church and its life (Acts 2:42–47; 4:32–37; 5:12–16) bears out this character: a society where no one calls any possessions his own, where all is shared in common, no one is in need, all persevere in the apostles' teaching, in the breaking of bread and prayer, where there is continual gladness, praise of God and favour with the people, where the apostles do wonders and signs and testify with great power to the Lord's resurrection. It is a community living, by anticipation, in the 'last days', as Luke tells us by inserting this phrase into the prophecy of Joel quoted at Pentecost (Acts 2:17); at the same time, or rather, perhaps, for that very reason, a community which constantly frequents the Temple, 'daily', 'with one accord'.

At this stage it is a group formed around the apostles. Of the Twelve, as individuals, Luke can tell us practically nothing except for Peter, their spokesman, and his silent and shadowy companion, John. Their presence in the story is symbolical rather than actual; but as symbolical witnesses to the twelve tribes of Israel they are of great significance. For the first seven chapters of Acts are concerned with the apostolic witness to Israel, by wonders and signs, especially the healing of the lame man at the temple gate, and by the preaching of the gospel. The people respond in great multitudes (Acts 5:14). They are God's people, Israel, as ready to believe the gospel as they were to listen to Jesus. It is with the false leaders of Israel that the confrontation lies, and this, despite Gamaliel's surmise that to oppose the apostles might be to fight against God himself (Acts 5:39), ends for the time being in the rejection of the apostles' witness by the high priest and the Sanhedrin, and the reproduction in Stephen's martyrdom of the trial and death of Jesus.

Throughout this first stage 'the church of Jerusalem' means the apostles: as leaders of an ideal community of the Spirit, and as witnesses whose testimony brings nearer the final hardening and rejection of the false Israel. After the persecution that follows Stephen's death the leaders of the Jerusalem church play a different role. Through scattering the church of Jerusalem this persecution paradoxically brings about a wide extension of the mission in Judaea and Samaria. The apostles, however, stay in Jerusalem. I do not think we need look for historical reasons why they should escape persecution: such as, that the persecution was directed only against Hellenist Christians, not against the Hebrew apostles. Luke's narrative here is not factually reliable, and indeed it is inconsistent, for only a short time later, when Saul returns from Damascus, there is a full-scale church in

Jerusalem, comprising disciples, brethren, and the Hellenist Barnabas, as well as the apostles. Luke simply believes that the apostles must stay in Jerusalem, for now that the Jewish hierarchy has remained impenitent, they are the true leaders of Israel. Just as the high priest sent out Saul with an anti-missionary commission to Damascus, so the apostles now direct and control the Christian enterprise from their own capital, Jerusalem, either personally or by sending envoys. But it seems that they do this, increasingly, as leaders of the Spirit-inspired church of Jerusalem rather than as 'the Twelve'. 'Twelveness' relates to Israel, not to the Gentile world. Hence after the Gentile mission has begun (following the repetition, for a Gentile group at Caesarea, of the un-mediated coming of the Spirit as at Pentecost, without wait-ing for the apostle, Peter, to act), the Twelve, as such, fade out of the picture. James the apostle is martyred, and there is now no need to make up the Twelve. Peter perhaps remains in Jerusalem after his deliverance from Herod's prison. The 'other place' to which he goes (Acts 12:17) need not be another city, and, three chapters on, he gets up at the Jerusalem council and speaks in a perfectly natural way which does not suggest that Luke means us to think he has returned from abroad. Luke may have shared the idea of Eusebius (*historia ecclesiastica*, 3.7.8) that the apostles remained in Jerusalem until the impenitence of the Jews was finally punished by the war with Rome. However this may be, Luke certainly thinks that the leadership passed to James and the elders, probably when Peter was imprisoned. He introduces this change most awkwardly: Peter simply tells the company at Mark's mother's house to report his escape from prison 'to James and the brethren'; and this is Luke's first mention of James. This suggests two things. That house was not, as has often been supposed, the headquarters of the Jerusalem church, for the leaders are elsewhere. More im-portant, Luke is not greatly interested in what individuals were now in charge at Jerusalem and what particular ecclesiastical office they held. The important thing for him is that they speak and act for the original and authentic Spirit-possessed church, now engaged in directing the ingathering of the Gentiles.

Before this, however, Philip's mission to Samaria, that great step forward to a new stage in the expansion of the Church, had been reported to the apostles in Jerusalem (Acts 8 : 14), and they sent their two leading men, Peter and John, not to administer Confirmation to the Samaritans, but to confirm their baptism by Philip, and to incorporate them, by the sign of solidarity, the laying-on of hands, into the community of the Pentecostal Spirit: so that the Samaritan converts, too, became a sort of extension of the Jerusalem church. Not that all converts everywhere had to be received in this way by the apostolic leaders. Philip was himself a Jerusalem missionary, one of the Seven; and his baptism of the Ethiopian, who was not a heathen but had been to worship at Jerusalem, needed no confirmation. But just as the revolutionary step of baptising Samaritans had to be investigated and ratified by Jerusalem, so did Peter's dealings with the Gentile household of Cornelius. After his almost episcopal tour (it is supervisory rather than missionary) of the churches established by unknown people at Lydda and Joppa, Peter is compelled by the direct action of God to acknowledge that Gentiles may receive the Pentecostal gift 'just like ourselves' (Acts 10:47). Once again, the news that the Gentiles had received the word of God was reported to the apostles and brethren. This time envoys are not sent; but Peter goes up to Jerusalem, and has to defend his actions under cross-examination by 'those of the circumcision' in the Jerusalem church (Acts 11:2). It is remarkable that the members of the church require an explanation from the chief apostle; he is accountable to the Jerusalem community, and only after he has told them about the divine interventions at

Joppa and Caesarea do they glorify God and admit that repentance has been given 'to Gentiles, too' (Acts 11:18). All this may suggest that the authority of the Twelve as such over, as well as representing, the Jerusalem church, was confined, in Luke's view, to those matters, namely, the tradition of the gospel events, which fell within the scope of their eye-witness testimony.

Meanwhile, Saul who, in the end, will go up to Jerusalem as a prisoner 'bound by the Spirit' (Acts 20:22), has been sent by the high priest, the head of the false Israel, to bring the true believers at Damascus, ironically enough, as prisoners, bound, to Jerusalem. His conversion brings with it a commission to witness before Gentiles, kings and the sons of Israel (Acts 9:15). Although this comes directly from the Lord, Saul's baptism and participation in the Spirit is mediated through Ananias. Ananias seems to have no connection with Jerusalem (how there came to be Christians in Damascus is left unexplained), though as one 'sent out' by the Lord Jesus (ὁ κύριος ἀπέσταλκέν με, Acts 9:17) he might almost be considered as a quasi-apostle. But in any case, in Luke's account, unlike Paul's own, attestation and recognition, one might almost say legitimization, follows very rapidly. Saul is introduced to the apostles as a body, becomes intimately associated with them, and does the same work in Jerusalem as Stephen, disputing with the Hellenists and only narrowly escaping Stephen's fate (Acts 9:27–29). Paul thus becomes, not an apostle in the full Lucan sense, but a close associate of the apostles and a representative envoy of the church of Jerusalem.

At Acts 11:19 Luke tells us how the dispersion from the Jerusalem church brought the gospel to Phoenicia, Cyprus and Antioch, and how at Antioch Gentiles were evangelized. Once again, this development is reported to Jerusalem. Luke seems not to allow the original apostles to travel further from Jerusalem than Samaria and Caesarea; they do not visit Gentile churches and supervise them in person (Luke knows nothing of Paul's dispute with Peter at Antioch). So Barnabas goes as the church's representative to inspect the situation (Acts 11:22f.). He legitimizes the Gentile mission at Antioch and authorizes Paul to join it. Luke also tells us of a visit to Antioch by prophets from the church of Jerusalem (Acts 11:27). It is not clear whether they are an official delegation; but the fact that such leaders as Paul and Barnabas are included in a list of 'prophets and teachers' at Antioch (Acts 13:1) suggests that they may be. At any rate, their visit evokes a great gesture of solidarity between this Gentile community and the mother church at Jerusalem. A collection is organized for the brethren there in view of an approaching famine, predicted by Agabus. It seems likely, as Haenchen suggests,[1] that Luke has transferred into this setting the material he found in his sources about the great Pauline collection for Jerusalem. The mention of Agabus may have been taken over from a tradition about Paul's last journey to Jerusalem, where the prophet reappears (Acts 21:10ff.). In reality, it was on that journey that the Gentile collection was brought to Jerusalem by Paul; but Luke may well have thought it fitting that the grand gesture of filial affection from the Gentiles to the focal point of that true Israel to which they had been admitted should be made at the very outset of the Gentile mission by the first major Gentile centre; and that the envoys concerned should be Paul and Barnabas. I doubt if Luke mentions the real Pauline collection at all. What is supposed to be a glance at it, Paul's statement before Felix that he had come to Jerusalem to give alms to his nation and offerings (Acts 24:17), may refer only to his acts of Jewish piety in the Temple concerned with the vows and sacrifices that he undertook.

The closing scene in this section of Acts which relates the beginnings of the Gentile mission is the solemn confirma-

[1] E. Haenchen, *Die Apostelgeschichte* (Göttingen, 1959), p. 322.

tion at Jerusalem by a council of apostles and elders, headed by James, with Peter, Paul, and Barnabas participating, of the incorporation of uncircumcised Gentiles into the Church. What Luke is interested in here is the recognition of the Gentile converts by the church of Jerusalem, despite the attempts of unauthorized people from Jerusalem to impose the rule of circumcision on them. This recognition is given on the ground that the scriptures attest God's intention to choose a people from the Gentiles, and because of the gift of the Spirit to Cornelius and his household.

I do not think that the phrase in the council's encyclical, 'it seemed good to the Holy Spirit and to us' indicates that the Jerusalem church believed itself to possess plenary inspiration. In fact, it probably means that the Spirit, by coming upon the Gentiles, made it clear to 'us' that we ought not to impose such a burden upon the converts; and we therefore testify to what the Spirit has thus shown us to be right. After this decision the church of Jerusalem sends a large delegation of leading men (ἡγούμενοι, Acts 15:22) to act like envoys of a Christian Sanhedrin and convey the council's letter to Antioch; and Paul and Silas go on to do the same in the region of Lystra and Iconium (Acts 16:4).

From this point onwards Paul operates more independently; but by means of the artificial device of 'missionary journeys' Luke keeps him in touch with Jerusalem. He and Silas set out carrying the decrees of the church, and later on, from Corinth, Luke brings Paul hurrying to a very brief visit to Jerusalem to greet the church (Acts 18:22), whether simply to report back after his tour in Europe or also to discharge his vow is not clear. This visit scarcely harmonizes well with the impression given by Paul's meeting with James on his final arrival at Jerusalem that he had been away from the city for a very long time.

There follows the regularization of Apollos, the Alexandrian Jewish missionary. This is done by Paul's associates in

what one might call the Jerusalem/Pauline mission, Priscilla
and Aquila, who bring Apollos within the ambit of that
mission. What his doctrinal deficiency was is not clear, but
it seems as though, being out of touch with Jerusalem, and
as it were a free-lance Christian, he could not share the witness of Jerusalem to the post-Ascension events and did not
know of the eschatological Spirit. So, when he is described
as 'fervent in spirit' this must be spelled with a small 's', and
mean, as in Romans 12:11, 'ardent' rather than 'inspired'. So,
too, at Ephesus, Paul gives baptism, such as the Jerusalem
church practised, to disciples, perhaps converts of Apollos,
who, like him, knew only John's baptism and had not been
touched by the Pentecostal Spirit. Like the Jerusalem
apostles at Samaria, Paul brings them within the Spirit-
possessed Church, and when he lays his hands on them, they,
too, speak with tongues and prophesy.

The last appearance of the Jerusalem church in Acts is at
Paul's final visit to the city. Like Jesus, Paul takes a firm
resolution to go to Jerusalem (Acts 19:21), and thence, he
knows, it is God's purpose that he should see Rome. Like
Jesus, he sends envoys ahead of him (Acts 19:22). Luke
knows nothing of the Pauline collection, supposes Paul's
long overland route to be due to Jewish plots to kill him
instead of being dictated by the organization of the collection, and presumably thinks that the seven representatives of
the Gentile churches who accompany Paul do so, not as
bearers of money but as signifying the fruits of the mission:
going up, as the prophets had said the Gentiles would go up,
to Zion. Since no collection is envisaged, why does Paul have
to go up, like Jesus, to Jerusalem? It must be because Luke
sees in this visit the decisive confrontation of the Jewish
leaders with the gospel. It reproduces the going up of Jesus
to Jerusalem, and Luke sees here both the vindication of Paul
as a strict observer of the Law and also the rejection by the
false Israel of its last chance to repent and avoid destruction.

Up to now the church of Jerusalem has borne its witness in the city and directed the gathering in of the Gentiles from outside. Now its part has been played. The theme of Luke–Acts has been the hardening in part of Israel and the inclusion of the Gentiles; and this story moves to its last act in Rome, possibly with the hint that for the future Rome is to replace Jerusalem as the centre and headquarters of the Church's mission.

Luke's picture of the apostolic age is very largely a theological reconstruction. He imposes a pattern on the early Church's mission, and this pattern is dominated by the idea of Jerusalem. It is not primarily a pattern of Church order. I doubt if Luke shares Clement's idea of the central importance of the appointment of the local ministries by the apostles and their continuation in due succession. Luke is not greatly interested in offices and office-bearers. He mentions local elders, presbyter/bishops, in the Gentile churches only in passing (Acts 14:23; 20:17, 28); and he is vague about the precise status of James and the Jerusalem elders, saying nothing about how these came to be appointed. Luke is interested, certainly, in apostolic succession, from Jerusalem to the churches of the Gentile world in later times; but it is neither a succession of ministerial order, nor a succession of orthodox tradition, to be maintained against Gnostic heresies, but rather a succession of witness to Christ, an apostolic testimony *in* Jerusalem to the self-styled leaders of Israel until they finally reject it, and an apostolic testimony *from* Jerusalem to Rome and the Gentile world of Luke's own day.